Finding My Voice Through the Words of My Father

MICHELLE BROWN

Published and distributed in the United States Michelle Brown. MichelleUniqueBrown, LLC. www.michelleubrown.com New York, NY.

Copyright © 2021 by Michelle Brown. MichelleUniqueBrown, LLC.
All rights reserved. No parts of this book be reproduced by any mechanical, photographic, or electronic process, or in the form of phonographic recording; nor may it be stored in a retrieval system, transmitted, or otherwise be copied for public or private use – other than for "fair use" as brief quotations embodied in articles and reviews – without prior written permission of the publisher.

The author of this book does not advice or prescribe any technique as a form of treatment for physical, emotional, or medical problems without the advice of a mental health professional, either directly or indirectly. The author intends to offer information of a general nature to help you in your quest for emotional and spiritual well-being. The author or publisher assume no responsibility for your actions associated with this book.

Certain names and other identifying information have been changed to protect and honor the innocent and those whose innocence has been lost, stolen, taken, or given away.

Book Coach – Robin Devonish
Cover Design – Okomota
Editing and Layout – Pen Publish Profit ™
Interior Design – Istvan Szabo, Ifj.
Cover and Back Cover Photo Headshot – Tina Burke Photography

ISBN 13: 978-1-7371359-0-6
LCCN: 2021908738
Printed in the United States of America

*God, you gave me the courage to write my testimony.
I am forever grateful for your unconditional love.
I thank you for being my father and protector throughout
this journey of finding my voice.*
- Michelle Brown

Acknowledgments

To the father whose drug addiction has caused you to abandon your daughter; I forgive you, I acknowledge you and I wrote this book for you. I want you to know that nothing is too hard for God. To the daughter that had to overcome abandonment and every unloving feeling that came with it; I love you, I feel your pain and I see your strength. I want you to know that I found my voice so that you could find yours.

To my mother Christine Brown, I thank you for your courage and for creating opportunities for me to be successful. You are loved, you are forgiven, you are blessed. You are an awesome Nana to your grandson, and I love you so much Mommy. To all my siblings, may God continue to bless and keep you. To my sister Hope, thank you for your support during some of the most difficult moments in my life. I love you. To my sister Star, thank you for being my best friend, keeping my secrets, giving me strength and encouragement during moments when I felt weak. Thank you for loving me through this journey. I love you. To all my amazing and beautiful nieces and nephews, aunty loves you all and may God continue to allow you to break down walls to access opportunity. You all will do great things! To my Nana, I love you. To all my aunties, uncles, and cousins, know that we are a strong family and God restores. I love you all.

To all my beautiful friends, thank you for believing in me, supporting me, encouraging me, and cheering me on. You all are so dear to my heart. I love you.

To my powerful book coach, Robin E. Devonish of Pen, Publish and Profit, thank you for your wholeheartedness. It has been a long journey with this book, but you understood me and my story. Your faithfulness to your purpose has encouraged me to be a self-published author. You spoke life into my fear and provided me with the tools to go forth. I thank you for guiding me along the way and pushing me to live a life of impact. I love you Robin!

To my Therapist Eric G. Glaude, your devotion and love for my family is greatly appreciated. You helped me own my feelings and showed me how to navigate through them in a healthy way.

To my family in Christ. Jesus changed the blood line! Kingdom Life Temple church in the Bronx, NY, thank you for having a church atmosphere that exudes God's word, welcome, love and family. I love KLT! To the Hunters and Hunters Ministries, my brother Sean, and my sister Shay, you are not only my spiritual family, but I call you, my friends. I thank you, my prayer warriors, for your commitment to my soul. Your prayers, labor of love and friendship does not go unnoticed. Thank you for helping me to find joy and laughter in my pain. I love The Hunters!

DEDICATION

My son, Ishmael Cleare Jr., I dedicate this book to you. Know that you are intelligent and courageous. I pray that my story empowers you to grow into a man of purpose. May God's favor always go before you. I love you so much son.

Michelle Brown

I was created in LOVE
My father just gave me my NAME
NEGLECT raised me
While I was mothered by PAIN
HOPE gave me the strength to weather the STORM
FORGIVENESS gave me my VOICE
and turned my cold heart warm

Introduction

As a child you learn how to utter your first words by mimicking the voice of your parents. It's like your voice lives inside of them. You share their sound, their beat, and their rhythm. You imitate the songs you hear them sing and copy their movements. This is how my parents began to introduce me to my voice. It was a creation of love. During a time when all things appeared to be complete and nurturing in an atmosphere for growth, a disturbing interruption took place that was so catastrophic it stopped my growth, silenced my voice, and broke my heart. I was four years old. I have been searching for my voice and the sound of my father's words since that moment.

Let me take you back to where it all began. My Mom is Christine Yvette Brown, and my Dad is Michael Eli Brown. My mother is the oldest of nine children. During her younger years she was raised by her grandmother in Philadelphia and later grew up in Harlem, New York City (NYC). My father was born and raised in Harlem, but his parents were from South Carolina. My parents met in Harlem in the summer of 1976. My mom was about twenty-six years old and had four children at the time. She was standing in the front of her building at 746 St. Nicholas Avenue while my Dad was walking his dogs. He absolutely loved dogs. My mom was light skinned with beautiful hair and a bright smile.

My Dad was tall, dark, and handsome. I would say they definitely looked good together and had that Harlem glow. In my Dad's eyes, he had to have her, and he made sure that he did.

I was told that the first six months of my parents' relationship was loving. My Dad was a nice guy and always included my Mom's children. Suddenly, things started to go downhill. Before I was born, my Mom was known to always be with her four children. My great grandmother was not fond of my father and did not allow him to visit her home because he started demanding my Mom's time away from her children. When he would visit, he would have to converse with my Mom in the hallway of the building. This created arguments between my parents and was the reason my Mom decided to leave her grandmother's home and move into my Dad's apartment on Convent Avenue. This move would soon pave the way to the beginning of turmoil for my family.

I am the youngest of my Mom's five children, two boys and three girls. I was her 80's baby. I was born on June 17, 1982 in New York Presbyterian/Columbia Hospital on Broadway, six years after my parents met. Prior to my birth, my father began dabbling with crack cocaine. The crack epidemic hit NYC in the early 80s. It flooded Harlem. During that time, you either sold drugs, used drugs or you sold and used drugs. My father chose to use and sell. Unfortunately, using got the best of him and he found himself fighting an addiction most of his life. My Mom and Dad got married Downtown in City Hall. Not only was my Dad a drug addict, but he also became extremely controlling, violent and abusive towards my Mom. His abuse caused her to be fearful and shattered her ability to mother in the loving way she was accustomed to.

My Dad's addiction to crack cocaine became severe around the time that I was one years old. My Mom along with my middle sister and I spent two years running from him to break free from his abuse. During this time, we moved from shelter to shelter throughout four boroughs of NYC. We rested in an abused women's shelter in Brooklyn, NY but he found us, and my Mom had to then transfer to a shelter in Queens, NY. We only were able to stay there for a short while because my Dad had located us again. I remember as we were leaving that shelter an elderly lady that worked there gave me a stuffed dog that I named Hildie. I still have that dog today. It is a reminder for me of where I've been, and it helps to keep me focused on where I want to go. Once we left this shelter, we were sent to the Roberto Clemente shelter in the Bronx, NY. Shortly after, in January of 1984, we were finally placed into a three-bedroom apartment on Loring Place in the Bronx. My older brothers were out in the streets most of the time. It was almost always my Mom, middle sister, and I together. The building we moved into was horrible. As soon as you entered the building a feeling of hopelessness smothered you. I turned three years old the year we moved into that apartment. There were broken stair rails and mailboxes, graffiti everywhere and empty crack bottles. I have seen drug addicts doing drugs in the hallway and dealers selling drugs in the lobby. Growing up there was scary and at times didn't feel like a home.

Meanwhile, my Dad was still running the streets and getting high. Sometime around 1985, my Dad decided to check himself into Phoenix House, which was a drug treatment program. During his treatment, my Mom attended counseling sessions with him as part of his recovery. During one of the sessions my mother was asked what she would do if my Dad ever became violent towards her again. My Mom said, she looked my Dad directly in the eyes and said out loud that she would kill him with her own hands.

My Dad stayed in Phoenix House for about eighteen months and completed the program. My Mom then allowed him to live with us. I remember feeling so safe when he came home. I did share a few funny moments with him while he was home. One of them was when he was asleep, I stuck a penny up his nose. I then got mad and started to cry because I wanted him to give me my penny back. It was buried in his nose so deep that my Mom had to help him get it out. My Dad was very tall, he would take me for walks outside and sit me on top of his shoulders, I remember feeling like I was on top of the world. There was a huge berry tree on the top of the hill on Loring Place. I could not believe that something so sweet grew in the middle of such a poor neighborhood. He would say to me as I sat tall on his shoulders, "Chell grab the berries, get it." I had to hand them to him because he knew which berries, I could eat and which ones I had to throw away. Another memory is when my Dad worked handyman jobs Downtown in rich neighborhoods that paid him good money. He would take me to work with him at times. I would see all his tools and believe that he was the smartest and strongest man on earth because he knew how to use every tool and could fix anything. He took pride in introducing me as his baby girl to people around the job. One day, I was even blessed to meet and shake the hand of the powerful Marian Anderson. You could not tell me as a little girl that my Dad was not somebody!

Sadly, the hilarious interactions, days of our berry walks, trips Downtown, and cool adventures would soon come to a halt six months later due to him suffering a relapse. My Mom found out he relapsed because he started behaving in a bizarre manner and began hallucinating which was creating hostility in the home. At this point, my Mom was no longer in love with him and thoughts of him did not consume her heart. My Mom gave him eleven years of her life and refused to allow him and his addiction to ruin her ladder years.

I remember the day like it was yesterday. My middle sister and I were home when my Mom and Dad got into an argument because he would not leave the house after being told by my Mom to go. Instead, he barricaded himself in the back room and refused to come out. My Mom then had to call the police so that he would be forced to leave. The police arrived and told my Dad that he must leave the apartment immediately and could return with them the next day to gather his belongings. When he returned with the police, his pride and addiction caused him to take everything in the apartment that he purchased. He took all the furniture, appliances, and televisions. We had a beautiful mauve color sofa set that he had just purchased for our living room. My teary eyes followed that sofa as it was being carried away. My middle sister was so hurt and angry that she threw her colorful handheld Simon game at him, that he brought her, while yelling "you want to take everything, take this too." When my Dad left, our place was close to empty.

I could recall thinking to myself, where did the love go? How could my Dad leave me with nothing? Over the next few days, we found out that he sold a lot of our furniture and items to people on our block in exchange for crack cocaine. This was the last childhood memory I had of my Dad because that was the last time, I remembered seeing him until I was well into my teens. When my Dad left that day, he did not say a word to me. I felt humiliated, abandoned, and unloved. I felt like an ant in a room full of elephants. My voice was being snatched away right in front of me and my heart was being torn in half.

My Dad left a void in me that created an angry silence, which over the years could only be expressed through writing. His absence forced me to journey through life in search of my voice, in search of something or someone to fill that void. Little did I know, my father shared the same love for writing and poetry. It seemed as if he was also searching for his voice and poetically writing his journey.

My Dad was more than an addict. He was a poetic writer with a passion for creating poems and stories in a way that painted pictures with words. He had a childlike imagination with an ability to take a reader into another world. At some point in his life and while I was a young girl, he ended up serving a few years in jail. During his times of incarceration or in his moments of solitude, he composed and mailed letters, poems, and stories to me. Sadly, my deep-rooted pain and unforgiving heart would not allow me to embrace his salutations. Therefore, most of his poems I did not read until I was an adult.

This book is my poetic response to some of my Dad's letters and poems. Not only is this book my reaction to neglect, pain, strength, storms and unforgiveness, it's my response to my Dad's love. I am sharing with you what I should have shared with my Dad back then as he wrote to me the thoughts of his heart. In this book you will experience my testimony as I take you through my journey of finding my voice through the words of my father.

Contents

Part 1. I Was Created In Love 1
Part 2. My Father Just Gave Me My Name 9
Part 3. Neglect Raised Me 13
Part 4. While I Was Mothered By Pain 29
A Moment Of Introspection 39
Part 5. Hope Gave Me The Strength To Weather The Storm 41
Part 6. Forgiveness Gave Me My Voice And Turned My Cold
    Heart Warm 45
Conclusion 53

PART 1.

I WAS CREATED IN LOVE

I knew that I was created in love, but I did not feel loved.

Dear Michelle,

I'll tell you another story not to short and not to long
In fact, my love it all started 9 months before you were born
I had the same name, you know Michael Brown
and your Mom's being my girl, at night she would come around
She wanted to get pregnant and said what do you want?
Don't lie, be true
I said, a cute baby girl, who looks just like you
She said, If I give you what you wanted, what would be her name?
I did not think she would have a girl, so I played the game
I said, Mychris or something close to Maria
But one thing was for sure it would not be Garcia
She said, I will tell you what we'll do
I will name the boy and the girl I will leave up to you
I said, ok I will grant you this child
She said, but all I ask is when she comes, you'll be there right beside me
I said, Mommy, are you really for real?
If so my Love, then you have got a deal

So now with that being settled, I started taking vitamins and working out
She would be pregnant soon, I had no doubt
Then one day I came home from work
As always, I ate dinner, played with the kids, and acted like a jerk
She said, guess what Honey
I am pregnant and looked at her tummy

Then for the next 8 months she thought I had other girls I bet
But the fact of the matter is I was too scared to have sex

One day your brother came and told me Michael, Mommy is in pain
I went running over there and found eighty dollars in the rain
I knew you were due, that was not fib
So, we used the money to buy you a new crib
I rushed in my car and ran all the lights
When we got there she was all rosey and calm
The doctor came out and said "sorry false alarm"
I gave her a kiss and she gave me a wink
But when I got home, I started to think

I gave her money to keep in case she ever needed to take a cab
She spent it anyway and made me mad
But I was around that night no doubt
Do you want to know what happened?
Well check this out
I was chillin in the house taking a shower
Your brother threw a rock at my window and almost broke the glass
He yelled "Mommy, the Baby" and was off in a flash
I jumped in my car and took off like a comet
But false alarm, no baby it was far far from it
When I pulled up, she was in front of her door
She said, 'the pain I can't take no more'
So, we were off again into the night
I don't have to tell you I ran every light
But we got there in the flash of an eye
I looked at her and said baby don't cry
She was bold and took the pain like a champ

I said, Chris I will be right back I must move the car
She Said, you better hurry up and don't go too far
When I got outside my car had blocked the whole street
I had already gotten five tickets that week
I found a spot around the corner that belonged to a truck
I said, thank you God and lady luck
By the time I got inside and found my girl
She looked stressed out, like she was from another world
I said, are you alright, baby are you in pain
She gave me a look like are you insane
I said, oh baby let me help you I'll do whatever I can
She said, don't do nothing just hold my hand
I held her hand and we bided our time

She was hooked up to machines like Frankenstein
One machine had a beep, one had a meter, and one wrote on paper
I figured one would blow up sooner or later
On one machine, I think the meter was for pain
She was twisting my hand like she was insane
Now the beep was for the baby, I think the baby's heartbeat
To me Michelle, you sounded so sweet
Now the machine that wrote on the paper was no joke
That is the one I think your Mama broke
I said, calm down Mommy don't push, let nature handle it
If you break that machine, I ain't paying for it
She said, Honey call the nurse because I really hurt
I said, then she will find out that the machine doesn't work

She sat up in bed and started to bend
Just then the nurse walked in

She checked Chris and left; I was glad she did not linger
She said, "not yet you are only three fingers"
Just as the nurse went out the door
Chris said, forget this I can't take no more
I pulled back the sheet and looked down
She said, go get the nurse my baby is coming now
I said, not now Chris just lay back and rest
She said, are you crazy this ain't no test
She yelled, Michael oh Michael this is for real
I yelled to the nurse THIS IS THE REAL DEAL
I ran back to Chris and held out my hand
So, when you came out you would have somewhere to land
and then you slipped out, the nurse came right on time because you
slipped into her hands, which were on top of mines
You were floating around in a bubble like a sack
I could see you clearly through it and you were looking back
She spread the sack tight on your face, it bursted then you and water came out
That was the first time you opened your mouth
You started to cry, stopped, and glanced at me
I had to move my head out of your face so that the nurse could see
She cleaned you off and put you in my arms
That's when I smiled and remembered your Mom
The nurse said "yes mother you have a Girl"
I said, yes and she is the prettiest girl in the world
I said, Baby she is so pretty and sweet
She said are you happy now, that you have your girl
I said, yes and she is the prettiest thing in the world
She said, thanks Honey for being here for this
I could not say nothing so I gave her a kiss

Finding My Voice Through the Words of My Father

It was 2:22 on the clock
There was one other thing I never forgot
As I kissed her and turned to walk away
She said, hey Honey HAPPY FATHERS DAY

Love Daddy
Michael E. Brown

This story is like music to my ears before the tears
LOVE created me
Dad, you wanted me to be your cute baby girl
while Mommy wanted you by her side to witness me enter this world
I could not imagine you two holding hands
LOVE doing its best
Healing, Supporting and Loving
How did life ruin this plan?

This story is like music to my ears before the tears
Dad, you said my heartbeat sounded so sweet
At 2:22, I was born inside of my water sack
Gift wrapped just for you
This type of birth is not normal but beautifully rare
You looked me in my eyes and thought about mom because you cared

I often wondered if LOVE stayed, what my life would be
Dad, I wanted you just as much as you wanted me
This story is like music to my ears before the tears
LOVE left me alone while the echo of my heartbeat fell on empty ears

Michelle

PART 2.

MY FATHER JUST GAVE ME MY NAME

My father knew that I was special. He wanted me to identify with him, so he named me at birth. However, his abandonment gave me an identity crisis.

Unique

You have proven to be priceless
Your value grows with time
Your style can never be copied
To me you are one of a kind

I cannot hide your beauty
Nor share it with a free heart
I admit being selfish and overprotective
I have always been that odd

Sometimes I am super intelligent
I love facing new goals
But to God and only you my dear
Can I even surrender my soul?

So, you see My Jewel
My richness in life
You have made my life complete
The name you have I love it true
and I am so glad it is Unique

Love Daddy,
Michael E. Brown

Daddy, If I am priceless and one of a kind
Why would you leave me in a world so cold?
If my style cannot be duplicated
Why do I feel that my value does not grow?

How can you be overprotective when you left me all alone?
With my beauty open to the world and no Dad to call
my own

I wish I could feel your loving soul
So I pray to God
that he returns you to me whole

I made your life complete
But you left me empty
You say I am your richness
But I feel like an impoverished child

You gave me the name Michelle Unique Brown because you loved me true
But I rather not have this name because I do not know you

Michelle

PART 3.

NEGLECT RAISED ME

Every missed birthday, holiday and school event reminded me that I was uncared for. Every day I walked home from school alone. I felt unprotected.

FINDING MY VOICE THROUGH THE WORDS OF MY FATHER

II

But Shell you see you are My Flesh + Blood. Just as much as you are your Mothers. And Because you are a part of me, I will not and can not even conceive a thought of any man, woman, animal, or machine to tell or order me when, where, or how I should relate to my child.

"Shell" let me try to explain a little better to you. I know you understand about Mommys and Daddys making Babys. Well Shell those Babys are Mommy's + Daddy's Blood Cells and little tiny peices of their Body's put together to make Babys. And for some one to tell me when I can or can' not see or talk to a part of my own Body.

14

is like saying To me "No" you can't Rub your Eye or wipe your Nose when you want to. only when They say So. And I Feel That's wrong, very wrong. I Have stayed Away From you This Long And will contiue Too only By choice. my choice Alone. I will Aways Abide By The Law But missing you The way I do I vsome Time's wonder will There Ever come a Time when I must Put my Faith And Trust in This man Made Law To A Reall Test, Behind A Lot of Memory's pain And Hurt How Far will I go or How Strong will I Be. Belive me I care Little About what your Mother wants or Feel's she Have. I do All I do now For you And you Alone. That's why I'll Get Noo For a certain Street Light.

Michelle I must close this letter now and I'm sorry Mommy won't except any more money from me for you. And I really don't know if I'll see you before, on, or after your birthday but you can believe until we meet again my love and best wishes travel with you.

By the way a Tooth Fairy came to my house looking for you a little while back, she said that she didn't know what house you may be sleeping in your Mommy's or mine. So she said she'll leave you a little money under both your house's bed pillows. So when I do get to see you I'll give you the money she left for you at my house.

    Love you very much. Daddy

Dad more than half my life you could not give me
what you had
Crack and cocaine were what you had
You left a fatherless daughter
wanting love so bad

                I started to hate you for what I did not have
                             In school you
                                were not there
                                      for
                            cupcakes with Dad
                  While kids were enjoying their cupcakes
            I was really sitting there just wanting my Dad
                I had to live with my pain and their pain,
                I'm speaking of my Mom and older siblings
              Which she had from previous relationships
          There was a moment where her pain was so deep
                            She seen you in me
                 so she told me I won't be nothing

Did your pride keep you away
because the circumstances were too tight?
I just want you to know that it was a cold summer for me that night
Your weakness did not allow you to fight for me and that is the truth
Did you tell the tooth fairy that you spent the money she left me for my missing tooth?

Finding My Voice Through the Words of My Father

> Dad more than half my life you could not give me
> what you had
> I had to hear it from
> my sisters how you
> beat Mommy so bad
> You left a fatherless
> daughter
> Wanting Love so sad

> Michelle

I had to take on a mission to go see someone that in every way imaginable has shown me that she doesn't love or want me any more.
So. Dear Wife for this Pain 5/22 I can say honesty along with you, (That you've done nothing) I've done it all myself...

When you asked "What's wrong" I really didn't know how to answer so I said "Nothing" Well now you know.
Honey I'm sorry But I'm not even ready to Deal with Michelle! Out of all the time I stayed in the park, she spends "total of" way be 15 min's with me, That hurts But I can understand she only a little girl and I've been out of her life so much that she really can't relate to missing me. Her friends right now and playing is more important. So I don't think me not being around will matter, "Not only that" after talking to her I've learned that to tell Mommy that she wants to see Daddy! She feels will make Mommy Mad. So she don't.
"Chris" There so many things about you NO matter how I look at them with us apart "Hurts". So I feel that I'll continue to stay away.

you can believe That I'm honestly happy to see
That you're happy and content, and everything is going
so well for you. Use have my Best Wishes + Blessing.

Before I close let me say That I'm not running
from you Because I Know That's not The answer,
You have Taught me Many things, and being
in love with you it has force me to learn
and change many things. I know in The
future I and many other people will
Thank you for The part you've played in
my life.
It's just That right now I can't see
any way awake or asleep to do without you,
and This life I live now is like another
Program That I can't Quit in. And I'm
force to live in ½ a hour at a time.
Perhaps God will hear my prayers one
of my many restless night's and End This
one sided love affair, and May be Then
I'll be able to stop unconsciously pushing
Every one else away from me, and Be like
you Content if not Happy.
I'll close now with out a I Love you
But I'll never forget That "Lady in The Plain Simple
Dress".
      For now and Maybe Forever
           Good Bye "Mommy"

Now you want to walk away from the only daughter you have
How could you leave me so suddenly?
It took fifteen minutes in the park of feeling unloved for you to determine that you had to leave
For years, a Dad's love did not exist to me
I thought I was the chosen one
You said, I was Unique
You said I was the prettiest girl in the world
But you left your little girl, who is one of a kind and more precious than gold
In a world so cold
I felt so confused
How could you choose
to not fight through your pain to prevent me from being wounded
Did you not know that a four year old
plays in the park because that is what children do?
Or was it just the selfish part of you
that wanted me to love only you?
What about me?
Maybe I played with my friends that day because I did not recognize the man in front of me
Where was the fight in you to see me through?
Where was the Dad in you that was supposed to provide and protect?
Instead, you allowed me to be raised by neglect

Michelle

Finding My Voice Through the Words of My Father

Hello My Love,

Write and tell me how you have been.
Are you ready for your next yarn to begin???

Did I ever tell you of the time I almost went to the moon?
Well have a seat in your house, maybe in your room.

One night your mother and I were dancing to old love songs.
Yes, them were the good old days, before you were born
We were playing around, we stayed up late
And a bulletin came on the radio, a news update
It said the test space shuttle was successful, that is how it began
Our next space trip will be very soon
We are hoping to try to put a man on the moon
I said baby did you hear that news update
I think it's a race between Russia and the United States
Now Chris was good at reading my mind you know
She said "no Michael, please don't go"
The next day I told the kids my plan
So, if I disappeared, they would all understand
After the kids, the only ones left that had to agree
Were my two German dogs named King and Arkee
I was going anyway the plan was in my head
So, it really did not matter what they said
I brought a book on space and studied it from the beginning to the end
Now I thought I was ready for this trip to begin
I got in touch with Washington, told them I was ready for the trip
What they told me back, really made me flip
They said, we have checked your records closely you see"

Yes, we know you have a GED!
We know you can read, right and do math too
Of course, you can hold your breath until you turn blue
Wait, Wait, Mr. Brown, This is Robert Dissen
I want you to stop talking now and try to listen

We understand Mr. Brown what this trip means to you
And how much you want to represent the red, white and blue
I want you to understand because I am your friend
Someone else was chosen for this trip, Captain John Glen
But don't worry this is not our last trip to the Stars
We'll be needing someone next year for our trip to Mars
I said, now this trip to the moon would have been fun
But going to Mars, now I aint that dumb

So, I slammed the phone down with my feelings hurt
Chris said, "hold your head up Honey, and go to work"
Your sister said, "don't worry Michael, I know you are one of a kind
You can drive me to school every day, I don't mind"
Your brother said, "so much for my future in stars"
Your other sister said, "I think yall both can make it to Mars"
Michelle, I never made the trip to become The First Man On The Moon
I pray you enjoy this Poem, I will write again soon

                        So long Daddy,
                        Love you Michelle
                        Michael E. Brown

Dear Michael,
I don't feel like calling you Dad

You are always asking me how I've been
as if the answer will ever be that I am ok
So might I ask, when you were getting high did it ever cross your mind that you and Mommy once danced to old LOVE songs?
Or did the smoke from that crack pipe
form a cloud in the image of Mommy to remind you to return home to the good old days?

Did you really want her and my siblings to think that you were taking a trip to the moon?
Did that hit really get you that high, so high that you thought you could walk on the moon?
What is the real truth inside this poem?

You did say that I was not born during the good old days
Well, that is true, because the only rhythm I witnessed you dancing to
were the sounds of your feet and fists kicking and banging against the apartment door
Yelling and screaming in rage for Mommy to let you in
Michael, do you know that I still jump from fear
when someone knocks on the door?
In fact, as a young girl, it took me about a whole year
to build up the courage to walk to the bathroom alone

But the irony of your poem
Describes you as not being chosen to take that walk to the moon
So, you slammed down the phone
Because you were hurt
Do you know what real hurt is?
Right by your side was Mommy encouraging you to hold up your head
The woman you chose not to LOVE but to hurt instead

You claim you were hurt though?
When in real life, today on June 7th
Your daughter, little me
Ten days away from turning eleven
I am sitting feeling hurt and disappointed
With my head hung low
No Dad to crown me as the birthday Queen
Over my bed I lean
And release a long sigh
Without my Dad right by my side
To use your hands to lift my head up high
So, to answer your question
This is how I've been

Michelle

Dear Michelle,

Hi Love, How are you?
I'm still doing fine myself! Oh before I forget
Let me tell you that I have enjoyed your last 5,000,000
Letters, (creep).

Let me ask you something else
Have you been enjoying Great Grandpa's poems?
Well, I'm sorry to say that I must bring them to an end, only because you have not written
And told me what you like reading about
I find it hard writing you poems not knowing if they are boring you or not

Believe me I wouldn't mind, if I knew, but I don't so I won't.
That does not mean that I'll stop loving or thinking about you

How did you like that last joke?
Or have you heard it before?
I have maybe another two months here, or less, before these people let me go
I don't know if I'll be here for the remaining time, or if they will send me closer to New York.
Either way, I'll be seeing you soon

Little Frouse, don't get me wrong, I know it's hard for you to sit down and write

And when you do, I know how forgetful you are as far as going to the mailbox
You may even have a letter in the mail to me now
I don't know, I guess you could say I am confused
Not worried, no where near worried, but I can't help to feel that something is wrong

I don't know, maybe I am bugging
I seem to be good at that
If so, then pay this letter no mind
Well so much for the facts of life
So, without further delay,
I am going to start the concluding chapter of your Great Grandpa Series of Poems
My wish is that you enjoy it

Love Daddy,
Michael E. Brown

Finding My Voice Through the Words of My Father

You wrote me this letter and began with asking
How am I?
You stated that you are fine with and exclamation point
I am so angry because I don't understand how you can be fine
After all this time
I spend days crying because you are not here
At times I think it's my fault and that you do not care
I am eleven and just finished fifth grade
While you are in jail
unable to witness my good grades

Instead of sending me these poems
trying to make me laugh
You need to write about the reason you chose crack over me
because all this superficial writing is annoying me

You said you are confused
Imagine how I feel!
I feel like a daughter that is always going to lose
You should feel as if something is wrong because your daughter is empty
and sings a sad love song
You should acknowledge the real facts of life
Like the night you left home chasing that pipe
Don't wish for me to enjoy your poems and stories
But pray you get your mind right
so you can be there for me

Michelle

PART 4.

WHILE I WAS MOTHERED BY PAIN

My mother made sure she provided me with all the tangible things I needed to be successful. She just was not able to treat my pain while she was burying her own.

Finding My Voice Through the Words of My Father

Last week I had a dream that I was taking a walk around this great big camp
You're not going to believe this, but in the dream, I found another magic lamp
Now this lamp was dull, dirty, and kind of cold
You couldn't read the writing on the side; it was just that old
A man then appeared in the dream
He was kind of short and very fat
He was dressed in orange and light green
And had the funniest pair of shoes I've ever seen
He had a double chin and hair the color of sand
He looked like the Penguin from the movie Batman
He said the lamp belonged to him and that he would allow me to make a wish
I said I have a wife and her name is Chris
She is short and kind of jolly, with eyes that make her cute
I was taking too long
So, he said, 'shoot'
What do you want son?
And what happened to you, how come you are a Bum
I said, I am not a Bum, you oversized whale
I've made a few mistakes that put me in jail
But I am learning from my mistakes, you piece of fat back
So, let's get to my wish, let's get back on track
He said, come on and give me your wish Young Buck
And watch your mouth, stop pushing your luck
I said, ok I've got a birthday wish but it must come from heaven
Straight to my baby at her age eleven

Love Daddy,
Michael E. Brown

Dad as I continue to read, I realize that you are really speaking about yourself
The only thing I can respect in this poem
Is the fact that you married my mom, yeah Christine is her name
You made her your wife
while she had four kids from prior relationships before I came
As I reference the man in your dream
My question is the same
What happened to you?
What caused you to get high and live like a bum?
I guess you asked yourself this question until you became numb
I see you acknowledge your mistakes that put you in jail
But I need to hear you admit that as a father you failed
You said that you are learning from your mistakes
I guarantee that on your release date you will be M.I.A
The only reason you have an address is because you are now property of the state
You really think you can put a smile on my face by sending me a birthday wish
You say it's from Heaven
But I know Heaven won't feel like this
It's too bad because at twelve a.m.
pain wished me a happy birthday as soon as I turned eleven
and reminded me to cry because my Dad's mistakes caused him to not be present
Today another birthday just came and went

Michelle

My Dearest Michelle,

How are you?

I'm well and pray you are much better.
I would like to ask you young lady, how does it feel knowing that you are not a little girl anymore?
When I think of you, I feel a change about to take place!
Not a bad one but a growing one.
One that all young girls must face sooner or later.
With Mommy's help, I think you'll be ready for it.
But enough about your body. Tell me about your plans.
I already know that every day that you live, you change a life for the better
So other than the lives you've already changed, what's your plans?
By the way, did you get your bike yet?
I have to close now, if I can get some stamps, I'll write again.

                        So long & I love you
                        Daddy,
                        Michael E. Brown

How does it feel knowing that I am not a little girl anymore?
I feel lost without a Dad around to make me feel adored
I wish you were here as my body changes
Do you know that men sometimes look at me as if I am grown?
Mommy alone cannot provide physical and emotional protection
How can she, when she is mothering me through pain that is causing her to be emotionally disconnected?
My plans should not include me writing you a penitentiary letter
Dad you must do better
No, I did not get my bike
Since you mentioned it, teaching me how to ride a bike would be beautiful
But most things that fathers do with their daughters
I am getting used to doing them without you

Michelle

Hi Michelle,

I'm growing old asking, how do you feel and not getting an answer.

But my mind, heart and feelings are telling me that you are fine
I myself, I'm well.
I went to the dentist last week and had four teeth pulled, my last four.
That might be why you have gotten so much Fan Mail,
I had to think a lot about you to deal with the pain.
But the pain had stopped now.
And since I have not heard from you yet, I am quite sure you'll understand if your
Letters stop, smile but not too hard.
I have sent you quite a few poems.
Let me know if you've got them all.
I wrote so many, I am really not sure but I think with these two that should make eleven. Counting the first one from The Rock, The Monkey....
I don't make copies; I write them as I think them up.
So let me know how many you have received.
I love you Michelle, write soon.

Love Daddy,
Michael E. Brown

It's interesting how I have grown to love writing poetry
I enjoy writing but I just can't seem to write to you
It is like a part of me believes that once you come out of jail
you will disappear from my life as usual
You are telling me that thinking of me helps you get through the pain from a dentist
But me thinking of you cuts my heart deep like a surgeon
Where do I begin?
What are your plans?
Are you using me to help you get through your prison time?
What's the count?
How many more days and a wake do you have on your mind?
Do you have plans for me when you come home?
Or will I receive a ton of empty promises with hugs and kisses?
All I want to do is to get good grades in school
So, I can make you and Mom proud
My dream is to take us out the ghetto and not having a Dad gave me a slow start
so I know it will take a little while
I work hard and push through my pain
I have so much to gain
A part of me is missing because you chose to indulge in a life of crack cocaine
God found a way to bless me with a similar gift as you
As a poet and the daughter of Michael Brown
I put my pen to my paper
In the most respectable way
I feel like your love I cannot gain
So, I rest in my tears as I write to stay sane
I am just a child being mothered by pain

Michelle

Finding My Voice Through the Words of My Father

Magic Man you are my master and I like you true
So listen closely to what you must do
I find your heart good and your love very strong
So believe me now, I'll tell you no wrong

I've seen you learn in your struggle for self
And the world made you king many day
Now look in the mirror, look good at yourself
And see what the man has to say

For it is not your father or mother or wife
Whose judgement upon you must pass
The fellow whose idea count most in your life
Is the one staring back from the glass

Some people might think you're a straight shooting chum
And call you a wonderful guy
But the man in the mirror, will say you're a bum
If you can't look him straight in the eye

He is the fellow to please, never mind the rest
For he's with you clear up to the end
And you've passed your most difficult test
If the guy in the glass is your friend

You may fool the whole world down the pathway of years
And get pats on the back as you pass
But your final reward will be heartaches and tears
If you have cheated the man in the glass

Now when I heard all this, about my life
I had no choice, except honesty to my wife
So, I went back and said, dig this Yvette
I can read but I can't write yet
I should have told you long ago
I'm sorry I didn't, but now you know…
(Sorry Chell, But my time ran out and I must go now.)

P.S. The part of this story about the mirror talking back, I've seen somewhere before. I just added it into your story because I thought that you might like to read something that once touched your Daddy's heart. So long Love.

Love Daddy,
Michael E. Brown

Dad I am a reflection of you
When I look in the mirror, I see your smile
I see your eyes
I see your frown
I am your child
When my mother looks at me, she sees you too
She sees the pain
She sees her truth
She sees the hurt
She sings the blues
The pain is so hard for her to bare
Her anger caused her to curse me while telling me that I will become nothing
Because you were not man enough to be there
I pray the man you see when you look in the mirror
Is a man that you could be proud of
I hope your purpose is clearer
I hope that man tells you to correct your wrongs
You have not been your best self for way too long
Dad you will lose your soul if the world is what you wish to gain
A brokenhearted woman is produced when she is mothered my pain
and you will lose your daughter if Mom's forgiveness is not obtained

Michelle

A Moment Of Introspection

As a young teenager I spent many nights in my room crying alone with just my paper and pen. I blamed myself for my father's addiction and often asked God was it something about me that caused my father to be absent. As the youngest child with brothers that were incarcerated for most of my childhood, I had no man in my life to fill the void left by my father or to show me big brother love. I was being mothered by a woman that gave me everything that I needed materially and financially but she was dealing with her own hurt and disappointment. My middle sister tried her best to be my protector, provider, teacher, and friend but she could not be my father. My father's absence left me to be raised by neglect and my mother's inability to be emotionally available caused me to be mothered by pain.

The pure love that I had for my father as a little girl turned into hate. I was angry. While growing up I often felt alone and misunderstood. My Mom did her best with what she had. Although she always reminded me that my Dad loved me and was not a bad person, I still did not feel loved.

I was not raised in church nor were my parents saved. I had no positive examples to follow to overcome poverty and struggle. Through my traumatic upbringing, in some strange way, I always felt God's comfort. Especially, when I realized that at a young age, he blessed me with a passion for writing. Writing helped me express my pain. It allowed time for me to introspect.

As I grew older, I found myself in unhealthy relationships with men that were like my father, my writing helped me to understand how I got there. My words, rhymes and metaphors gave me a sense of identification and an explanation of who I was becoming.

Part 5.

Hope Gave Me The Strength To Weather The Storm

Through all the hurt and disappointment, I still dreamed of a relationship with my father. His words gave me hope, they made me strong.

My Wish

6/17/97

Over the year's
God has answered Request "I call Wish",
And althought They numbered in The Thousand's
  Not one did he miss.
Your intelligence's, your look's you ability
  Were all apart of My Request,
So as I sit now, I think and write
  Making This Wish one of My Best.
I wish you Love, Peace, happiness
  For many year's To come,
I wish you Luck, Safety, and Success
  All while having Fun.
I wish you Compassion, Patience, and understanding
  In all you say and do,
I wish you Power, strenght in handeling
  The Task's life has set for you.
I wish you ... o happy Birthdays
  Each one "Love" From Mother and Me,
I wish you another Million happy Day's
  Being all That you can Be.
It isn't often I make a Wish, shareing Thing's I say
But if This is Truly answered, you'll be
Granted a happy Birthday.
I'll say so long to you now
And I'll say it with a Kiss,
All because I love you true Michelle
I've share'd with you "My Wish" W.E.B.

Over the years God has answered my prayers I called Hope
Although they number in thousands, I prayed "I hope to see my Dad" the most
I need you close
Especially today on my birthday there is so much I want to say
I have a boyfriend whom I think I love
He tells me sweet things but deep down inside I refuse to accept it as true
All because the things he says I have never heard them from you

A Dad is a girl's first love who gives his daughter an example of how to be loved by a man
So, I am trying to receive your Godly birthday wish with an open heart and open hand
I can't lie this is very hard to do
Because the first man to hurt me was you

I can't help but cry hearing my Dad express how smart I am
And how you honor my beauty and ability
Your birthday wish is helping me to see how a man is supposed to love me

All these years I shut down because of your neglect
But today my heart and arms are open
Leaving room for you to Bless

Dad, I want you to know how your words strengthen me
They speak power and blessings into my life

I need you to come home because I am ready to allow you to turn your wrongs into rights
This birthday wish was the hope I needed to help me fly above life's storms
The expression of your love is mending pieces of my heart that was once torn

Michelle

PART 6.

FORGIVENESS GAVE ME MY VOICE AND TURNED MY COLD HEART WARM

I did not forgive my father for him; I forgave him for me. Unforgiveness caused me to forget my father's sound, his beat, and his rhythm. It blocked the memory of him teaching me my voice. Forgiveness allowed my cold heart to feel and gave me the authority to speak.

My Dearest,

Forgive Me

There are no words to say I am sorry for all the things I have done
There is no way to go back in time and turn our sad times into fun
But there is one thing that I can do that would make you proud of me
From this day forward show you love and be all that I can be

                                        Love Daddy,
                                        Michael E. Brown

As you laid in your sick bed suffering from a liver disorder caused by years of drug abuse
You gazed into my eyes
As I looked at you fight against death
Just to allow me, your baby girl, to see the twinkle in your eyes
Along with your bright warrior smile
Only I had that effect on you
So, I smiled right back only to allow you, my Dad, to see
That even though your liver failed and you weighed about 100 pounds
You were not defeated
I made sure my smile gave you every reason to believe it
I wanted you to know that you were my Champion
You were so proud of me, but I was prouder of you
Because you fought hard and overcame your struggle with addiction
But fought even harder for my love
Never forgetting
To let me throw my blows without gloves
Never dodging my jabs and right hooks
Instead, you allowed me to hit you
Because you knew in your heart that I expected you to leave me again
So tonight, in my eyes you won Daddy
Because you won
I now know that I am a winner
I only wish I could tell you this

Michelle

Finding My Voice Through the Words of My Father

You left when I was about five years old
I tried to remember the details of your face as I created an image
in my mind that met the description I was told
But that image was blurry and colorless
As time passed, months turned to years the image began to disappear
As a little girl, every time I saw a homeless black man on the street I would stare
at his face and say to myself, that might be my Dad
But no one never stared back
I could remember feeling so empty and real sad
I knew you were addicted to crack and when you left, I figured you was living homeless on the street
Picking out of garbage cans for food to eat
Mom and I had no clue where you could be
Until I received a letter from you with an address belonging to a NYC department of corrections facility

As a grown woman and a mother to a son
I sit here today reading your short stories and poems
which were written to me so beautifully
Tears are streaming down my cheeks
I wish I knew then what I know now
You loved me so much back then just as you do now
Daddy I never knew you cared
For months and years, you continued to write me from Rikers Island, one of the nation's worst prisons, In spite of me never given
you a written
Dear Dad reply

It amazes me how in most of them you chose to write in third person
using rhythmic words and metaphoric characters
as you narrated your journey of becoming A Man, A Father, A Husband and An Addict
I have to read them over and over because each time I learn something different about your good and bad habits
Including your discovery of who you were and who you hoped to be

I am reading one written to me on my birthday, June 17, 1993
It was a humorous poem because you wanted me to know that it was your desire to gift me with laughter
Till this day all those that know me know that I crave for a good laugh so in that poem you gave me the best birthday gift ever

Daddy I wish I knew then what I know now
because I would have simply replied with a thank you note attached with a smile
I still think about the years we spent together before you passed
And how both of us, so loud and so frequent we would just laugh

I truly wish I knew then what I know now
the drug addict father you were in 87
was a temporary setback that had to happen
It was designed to prepare you to be a father drug free for over 20 years,
You looked me in my face and apologized for not being there as we both wiped away our tears
You were an exceptional grand-dad

your grandson never had to experience you
strung out on crack
and I honor you for that
If I would have known then what I know now
Daddy, I would have forgiven you sooner
I would have written you back.

Sorry

Michelle

Blossom

*You have changed many things
On this planet called Earth
And the changes started
That day of your Birth
I could tell when you began
To make people smile
Receiving compliments and flattery
At the age of a child
But now that you are an adult
The world is not the same
And society worldwide
Also view my claim
I feel successful and proud
Knowing I've done my Deed
And I thank God for you
My Precious Seed*

*Love Daddy,
Michael E. Brown*

Finding My Voice Through the Words of My Father

Dad, You have changed many things
On this planet called Earth
And the change started
That day you acknowledge my hurt

Dad, I could tell when you began
To make me smile
Receiving compliments and flattery
As you bragged about your first grandchild

Dad, but now that I am older
The world is not the same
And society worldwide
Is enduring lots of pain

I feel successful and proud
Knowing I've done my deed
And I thank God for You Dad
That I was chosen to be your precious seed

Dad, as the sun shines and flowers bloom
My warm heart fills this room
Our story of forgiveness and reconciliation is
written for the world to know
Your poetic words gave me my voice
I am ready to Blossom
I am ready to grow

Michelle

Conclusion

God said in Jeremiah 1:5 *"Before I formed you in the womb I knew you, before you were born I set you apart; I appointed you as a prophet to the nations."* Although I was not raised in a house that encouraged a relationship with God, this scripture explains why I felt God's presence with me growing up. He formed me and you. He knew what we were going to endure as children, teenagers, young adults and as grown women and men. He gave me an outlet to release the pain even though I could not verbally express it at the time. As I grew into my twenties my heart was becoming tender and ready to receive Jesus Christ as my Lord and Savior. He began circumcising my heart and preparing the way for me to reconcile with my father.

My father came out of jail, completed a drug treatment program and was clean for years before he committed himself to a relationship with me. We would have small talks over the phone, but I was not ready to connect with him. However, God had a different plan. I knew the day would come when we would have to have our difficult conversation. We talked right before I was about to attend college. I went to his small apartment in Harlem, sat in his living room on his couch, faced him and began to pour out my heart.

The tension in the room was so thick I could remember us feeling so afraid of rejection and excuses. But we chose to stay present in the moment. I yelled, I cried, and I displayed so much anger towards him in that moment. I was waiting for him to take flight. I was almost saying things to force him to take flight, but he would not flee. He sat there in a posture that was pleading for my forgiveness. He listened and promised that he will never leave me again. This time I heard a difference in his voice. I watched this grown man cry as he uttered the words I needed to hear, which were "Michelle I apologize, please forgive me." He did not give me excuses; he admitted his wrongs. This time he was ready to be my Dad. At that moment, my wall began to crack. I felt vulnerable and ready to receive the love I always waited and hoped for. We were prepared for God to reconcile our relationship. This was a breaking point for us. This was the beginning of our healing process. This conversation was the major conduit for us experiencing the power of reconciliation. Our lives were never the same.

This breakthrough was the reason I invited my Dad to my college graduation. I was receiving my undergraduate degree with a bachelor's in business administration. I knew that I wanted him to be there. I wanted to share this moment with him, and I wanted to know what it felt like to make my Dad proud. I could remember seeing how happy and appreciative he was. He showed up like a professional photographer. There were moments when I would catch him staring at me in awe. He gazed at me like I was the most beautifullest woman in the room. He took photos of me like I was the most valuable thing his camera ever captured. He honored me like I was the smartest person graduating. I knew on that day that I wanted my Dad, I needed him. On that day I knew and felt my value by looking into his eyes and embracing his gestures of love.

God saved me in my early twenties and had already blessed me with the power to forgive. Unbeknownst to me, God was preparing me for a life without my natural father. I did not know, but God knew that seven years later, on December 04, 2011, my Dad would pass away and that I would later read his poems and stories that were written to me. I did not know that these stories would give me more profound healing, insight and understanding.

Psalms 27:10 says, *"Though my father and mother forsake me, the Lord will receive me."* Like me, you too may know God as your Savior, Healer, Redeemer and much more, but God wants us to truly know him as our Father, as our Dad. As women, I believe that we were created with a need to feel protected and provided for. Our Dads are the first men that we expect this from. When our Dads do not live up to this expectation our image of them becomes tainted and we build up a wall of resentment. God knew that my wall needed to be broken down so he orchestrated the reconciliation between my Dad and I so that I can receive Him not only as my Savior but as my Dad and Divine Protector.

After traveling with me through this poetic expression of my healing process, I hope you realized that life is a journey and not a race. As children we do not get to choose our parents or the circumstances that surround us when we enter this world. Oftentimes, your journey may cause you to travel a long distance through dangerous and difficult circumstances. As a girl and even as a grown woman, I felt vulnerable and defenseless. There were times in my life when I was in danger and yearned for my father's protection. I know you may also face situations that cause you to feel weak and unprotected. I want you to know that on your journey you may encounter love, neglect, pain, strength, storms and unforgiveness, but keep traveling and make sure to move at your own pace. You are competing with no one. Your only purpose should be to become a better version of yourself while impacting the life of someone else.

I hope this book encouraged you to embark on your journey of healing yourselves and your relationships with your family through the power of forgiveness and reconciliation. Allow God to reconcile your broken relationships with your parents so God can receive you to Himself as whole. You deserve to heal, to find your voice and to walk in your value. Let God help you heal your pain so that you can let it go. I further encourage you to take a moment to use the blank sheets in the back of this book to create a poem or letter from your heart. Release all of the things you've wanted to say to your father and allow God to do His healing work.

I found my voice through the words of my father. I now see myself as Christ sees me and I am intentionally walking in my purpose. You can too. You are powerful. I encourage you to take a moment to use the blank sheets in the back of this book and create a poem or a piece of writing from your heart to God's ears. Write your pain, disappointments, trials, victories, desires, and moments of growth. Turn your hurt into something empowering. Read your words out loud. Then decree and declare that the situations that were designed to silence your voice will be used by God to amplify your voice to impact others. You are powerful.

Just Shells

Perhaps after reading this book, you feel led to use your voice and communicate with your father. If he is with us, I encourage you to write a letter and share. If he is no longer with us, write a letter anyway. This exercise and the use of the following writing prompts will be therapeutic and will give you an empowering push to find your voice.

Dear Daddy, I hope...

Finding My Voice Through the Words of My Father

Finding My Voice Through the Words of My Father

Dear Daddy, I want...

FINDING MY VOICE THROUGH THE WORDS OF MY FATHER

Dear Daddy, I feel...

Finding My Voice Through the Words of My Father

Finding My Voice Through the Words of My Father

Dear Daddy, it hurt me when...

Finding My Voice Through the Words of My Father

Finding My Voice Through the Words of My Father

Dear Daddy, I forgive you for...

Finding My Voice Through the Words of My Father

Finding My Voice Through the Words of My Father

www.ingramcontent.com/pod-product-compliance
Lightning Source LLC
Chambersburg PA
CBHW072206100526

44589CB00015B/2396